PUNCTUATE IT!

HYPHENS AND DASHES

BY KATE RIGGS

ILLUSTRATED BY RANDALL ENOS

CREATIVE EDUCATION • CREATIVE PAPERBACKS

Published by Creative Education and Creative Paperbacks
P.O. Box 227, Mankato, Minnesota 56002
Creative Education and Creative Paperbacks are
imprints of The Creative Company
www.thecreativecompany.us

Design and production by Liddy Walseth
Art direction by Rita Marshall
Printed in the United States of America

Library of Congress Cataloging-in-Publication Data
Riggs, Kate.
Hyphens and Dashes / by Kate Riggs; illustrated by Randall Enos.
p. cm. — (Punctuate it!)
Includes bibliographical references and index.
Summary: An illustrated guide to the punctuation marks known as hyphens
and dashes, including descriptions and examples of how to properly use them
to join words together in sentences.
ISBN 978-1-60818-734-8 (hardcover)
ISBN 978-1-62832-330-6 (pbk)
ISBN 978-1-56660-769-8 (eBook)
1. English language—Punctuation. 2. English language—Usage.
3. English language—Clauses.

PE1450.R53 2016
428.2/3—dc23 2016002553

CCSS: L.1.2; L.2.2; L.3.1, 2, 3, 4, 5; L.4. 1, 2, 3, 4; RI.3.1, 2, 7, 8; RI.4.2, 8

First Edition HC 9 8 7 6 5 4 3 2 1
First Edition PBK 9 8 7 6 5 4 3 2 1

TABLE OF CONTENTS

2
3
4
5

INTRODUCTION

"ON YOUR MARK–GET SET–GO!" YOU TAKE OFF DOWN THE WELL-WORN TRACK. YOUR SHOES MAKE A THUMPING SOUND. THE 100-METER DASH IS USUALLY YOUR BEST RACE. BUT YOU CAN FEEL SOMEONE IS ABOUT TO PASS YOU. YOUR FEET CROSS THE FINISH LINE AT ALMOST THE SAME TIME. A FIRST-PLACE RIBBON IS YOURS!

WORKING TOGETHER

Hyphens and dashes are sneaky punctuation marks. Those lines in midair may look similar, but they do different things. What they have in common is that they join words together. Hyphens link individual words together. Dashes link words within a **sentence**.

Hyphens are often used with certain types of words. A compound word is formed when two or more words are joined together. Hyphens connect parts of some compound words, making hyphenated compounds.

The merry-go-round was broken at recess.

Other types of compounds do not use hyphens. These are called open compounds and closed compounds. You can always check a dictionary for how to

spell compound words!

Common hyphenated compounds include age terms and some color words. If you are nine years old, you might describe yourself as a "nine-year-old child." Maybe you like the color pinkish-purple. These same terms might not always be hyphenated.

PUNCTUATION PRACTICE:

Can you tell which words are compounds, just by looking at them? There is one of each type in the sentence below.

In third grade, I got a stomachache from riding the tilt-a-whirl.

A: open compound: third grade; closed compound: stomachache; hyphenated compound: tilt-a-whirl

HYPHENDASHYPEN+DASH
TILT
HYPHENDASHYPHEN

BEFORE OR AFTER?

Another thing to keep in mind about hyphens is the **part of speech** they go with. Adjectives are words that describe nouns. Adverbs describe verbs. Hyphens attach certain words to make adjectives. They also attach some adverbs to verbs in the past tense. Let's look at the adjective *well* first:

Graham's team had a well-earned win last night.

The win was well earned.

The noun *win* is in both of those sentences. When the adjective (*well*) comes before the noun, it gets hyphenated. But in the second sentence, *well* comes after the noun. This time, the compound

well earned stays open.

Many adverbs end in –*ly*. That's usually how you can tell they're adverbs! But some do not have that ending. *Best*, *most*, *worst*, and *much* are some of the most common. These adverbs may take a hyphen when they come before a noun.

The best-prepared goalie gets to play in the finals.

What if the example above did not use a hyphen?

The best prepared goalie gets to play in the finals.

You might not understand that there are two words describing "goalie." The hyphen lets you know that those words belong together. And they both describe the noun. A compound of an adverb ending in *–ly* plus an adjective or other word never needs to be hyphenated. The *–ly* tells you that the next word is another descriptor.

PUNCTUATION PRACTICE:

You know how to recognize adverbs. You even know a few that do not end in *–ly*. But can you tell when word pairs need a hyphen? One sentence at right needs a hyphen. Remember to find the noun first!

1) The most improved runner gets to join the relay.

2) The runner who is most improved gets to join the relay.

A: 1) The most-improved runner gets to join the relay.

THAT'S DASHING!

The em dash is usually what people mean when they talk about a dash. Dashes are used for emphasis. They may also set off words that offer more explanation. They are like colons, commas, and parentheses that way. But using a dash gives a different meaning to your sentence.

What do you notice about the following sentences?

Molly, the team's best shooter, made four baskets.

Molly (the team's best shooter) made four baskets.

Molly—the team's best shooter—made four baskets.

When "the team's best shooter" is surrounded by commas, it sounds pretty calm. You're stating that Molly is the team's best shooter. Putting those words in parentheses means that it's not important to know that. The dashes make a big deal out of it, though! They make you pause for that thought.

PUNCTUATION PRACTICE:

Where would you put dashes in the following sentence? Look for the words that could be extra information.

Sam who set a record last time ran in the fastest heat.

A: Sam—who set a record last time—ran in the fastest heat.

100 M

BREAKING APART

Learning how sentences are built from nouns, verbs, adverbs, and adjectives is a key part of understanding punctuation. Hyphens and dashes break words apart.

Yet they also bring them together. They are important members of the punctuation team!

-ACTIVITY-

COMPOUNDING MATTERS

Open compounds are spelled as two or more words. Closed compounds are two words that have become one. And hyphenated compounds use hyphens in between the words. Look for all those types of compounds in the following sentences. Are they used correctly?

The eight-year-olds used all the balls at recess.

A: The hyphenated compound is correct.

Our uniforms are reddish brown this year.

A: The open compound is correct because the words "reddish brown" do not come before the noun.

The team will meet at the north east corner of the field.

A: "Northeast" should be a closed compound because compass points and directions are always closed—unless three directions are combined (as in "east-northeast").

Maria took a half-hour to walk the 100 meter race.

A: The hyphenated "half-hour" should be an open compound because it is a noun. The open "100 meter" should be hyphenated because the number and noun work together as an adjective.

GLOSSARY

part of speech: a word that plays a certain role in a sentence; some main parts of speech are nouns, verbs, adjectives, adverbs, pronouns, prepositions, and conjunctions

sentence: a group of words that has a noun as the subject and a verb

READ MORE

Bruno, Elsa Knight. *Punctuation Celebration*. New York: Henry Holt, 2009.

Truss, Lynne. *Twenty-odd Ducks: Why, Every Punctuation Mark Counts*! New York: G. P. Putnam's Sons, 2006.

WEBSITE

Grammar Blast

http://www.eduplace.com/kids/hme/k_5/grammar/

Test yourself on what you know about sentences and other punctuation.

Note: Every effort has been made to ensure that the website listed above is suitable for children, that it has educational value, and that it contains no inappropriate material. However, because of the nature of the Internet, it is impossible to guarantee that sites will remain active indefinitely or that their contents will not be altered.

INDEX